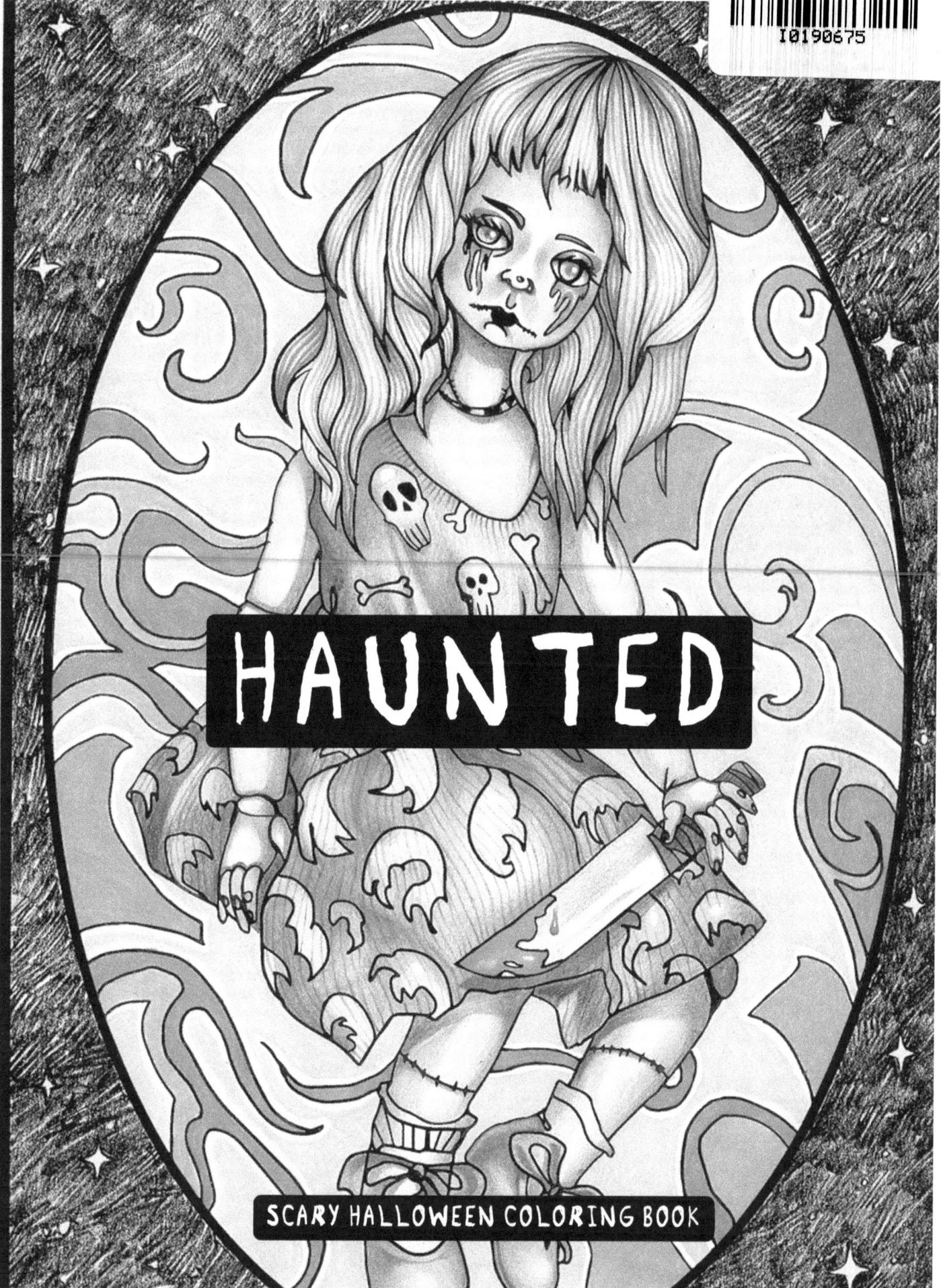

HAUNTED

SCARY HALLOWEEN COLORING BOOK

LIGHTBURST

MEDIA

LightBurst Media
www.lightburstmedia.com

Hi.

We are glad you have decided to embark on a coloring adventure with Haunted: Scary Halloween Coloring Book.

It is recommended that you use colored pencils to color the images. If you use another medium, such as markers or gel pens, you can place a blank sheet underneath the page you are coloring. There are extra sheets of paper in the back of the book that you can use for this purpose or to test out color combinations.

We invite you to join our mailing list at lightburstmedia.com. When you join, we will send you five free coloring pages. In addition, you will be the first to receive updates and free coloring pages from our future coloring books.

We would *greatly* appreciate you leaving a review for Haunted and sincerely hope that it provides you with many hours of enjoyment, relaxation, and fun!

Color Your Dreams,
Bonnie Bright
LightBurst Media

SHOW US YOUR FINISHED COLORING PAGES!

** t**

@lightburstmedia

f

www.facebook.com/lightburstmedia

lightburstmedia

#lightburstmediacoloring

Send us your completed work and we will proudly share it on our feeds!

You can also email us your feedback, suggestions, completed work, etc.

We love to hear from you.

FEEDBACK@LIGHTBURSTMEDIA.COM

FASHION FORWARD

1960s Fashion Coloring Book for Adults

SPACE DREAMS

SCI-FI Adult Coloring Book Adventure

Other

LIGHTBURST
MEDIA

Coloring Books!

BACK TO THE 80S

1980S FADS AND FASHION COLORING BOOK FOR ADULTS

GROOVY 70S

DISCO

FASHION COLORING BOOK FOR ADULTS

www.ingramcontent.com/pod-product-compliance
Lightning Source LLC
Chambersburg PA
CBHW081221020426
42331CB00012B/3063